Jack Straw's Castle

THOM GUNN

Jack Straw's Castle
and Other Poems

FARRAR, STRAUS AND GIROUX   NEW YORK

First published in 1976 by Faber & Faber Limited
First American printing, 1976
Printed in the United States of America

Library of Congress Cataloging in Publication Data
Gunn, Thom.
    Jack Straw's castle and other poems.
    I. Title.
PR6013.U65J34   1976   821'.9'14   76-40937

To the memory of
Tony White

Contents

3.

I

The Bed

The pulsing stops where time has been,
 The garden is snow-bound,
The branches weighed down and the paths filled in,
 Drifts quilt the ground.

We lie soft-caught, still now it's done,
 Loose-twined across the bed
Like wrestling statues; but it still goes on
 Inside my head.

Diagrams

Downtown, an office tower is going up.
And from the mesa of unfinished top
Big cranes jut, spectral points of stiffened net:
Angled top-heavy artefacts, and yet
Diagrams from the sky, as if its air
Could drop lines, snip them off, and leave them there.

On girders round them, Indians pad like cats,
With wrenches in their pockets and hard hats.

They wear their yellow boots like moccasins,
Balanced where air ends and where steel begins,
Sky men, and through the sole's flesh, chewed and pliant,
They feel the studded bone-edge of the giant.
It grunts and sways through its whole metal length.
And giving to the air is sign of strength.

Iron Landscapes
(and the Statue of Liberty)

No trellisses, no vines
                 a fire escape
Repeats a bare black Z from tier to tier.
Hard flower, tin scroll embellish this landscape.
Between iron columns I walk toward the pier.

And stand a long time at the end of it
Gazing at iron on the New Jersey side.
A girdered ferry-building opposite,
Displaying the name LACKAWANNA, seems to ride

The turbulent brown-grey waters that intervene:
Cool seething incompletion that I love.
The zigzags come and go, sheen tracking sheen;
And water wrestles with the air above.

But I'm at peace with the iron landscape too,
Hard because buildings must be hard to last
—Block, cylinder, cube, built with their angles true,
A dream of righteous permanence, from the past.

In Nixon's era, decades after the ferry,
The copper embodiment of the pieties
Seems hard, but hard like a revolutionary
With indignation, constant as she is.

From here you can glimpse her downstream, her far charm,
Liberty, tiny woman in the mist
—You cannot see the torch—raising her arm
Lorn, bold, as if saluting with her fist.

                       Barrow Street Pier, New York
                       May 1973

The Corporal

Half of my youth I watched the soldiers
And saw mechanic clerk and cook
Subsumed beneath a uniform.
Grey black and khaki was their look
Whose tool and instrument was death.

I watched them wheel on white parade grounds.
How could the flesh have such control?
Ballets with symmetry of the flower
Outlined the aspect of a soul
Whose pure precision was of death.

I saw them radiate from the barracks
Into the town that it was in.
Girl-hungry loutish casanovas,
Their wool and webbing grated skin
For small forgettings as in death.

One I remember best, a corporal
I'd notice clumping to and fro
Piratical along my street,
When I was about fifteen or so
And my passion and concern was death.

Caught by the bulk's fine inward flicker,
The white-toothed smile he turned to all,
Who would not have considered him
Unsoldierly as an animal,
Being the bright reverse of death?

Yet something fixed outlined the impulse.
His very health was dressed to kill.
He had the acrobat's love of self
—Balancing body was his skill
Against the uniform space of death.

Fever

Impatient all the foggy day for night
   You plunged into the bar eager to loot.
A self-defeating eagerness: you're light,
   You change direction and shift from foot to foot,
Too skittish to be capable of repose
   Or of deciding what is worth pursuit.

Your mother thought you beautiful, I suppose,
   She dandled you all day and watched your sleep.
Perhaps that's half the trouble. And it grows:
   An unattended conqueror now, you keep
Getting less beautiful toward the evening's end.
   The boy's potential sours to malice, deep
Most against those who've done nothing to offend.
   They did not notice you, and only I
Have watched you much—though not as covert friend
   But picturing roles reversed, with you the spy.

The lights go up. What glittering audience
   Tier above tier notices finally
Your ragged defeat, your jovial pretence?
   You stand still, but the bar is emptying fast.
Time to go home babe, though now you feel most tense.
   These games have little content. If you've lost
It doesn't matter tomorrow. Sleep well. Heaven knows
   Feverish people need more sleep than most
And need to learn all they can about repose.

The Night Piece

The fog drifts slowly down the hill
And as I mount gets thicker still,
Closes me in, makes me its own
Like bedclothes on the paving stone.

Here are the last few streets to climb,
Galleries, run through veins of time,
Almost familiar, where I creep
Toward sleep like fog, through fog like sleep.

Last Days at Teddington

The windows wide through day and night
Gave on the garden like a room.
The garden smell, green composite,
Flowed in and out a house in bloom.

To the shaggy dog who skidded from
The concrete through the kitchen door
To yellow-squared linoleum,
It was an undivided floor.

How green it was indoors. The thin
Pale creepers climbed up brick until
We saw their rolled tongues flicker in
Across the cracked paint of the sill.

How sociable the garden was.
We ate and talked in given light.
The children put their toys to grass
All the warm wakeful August night.

So coming back from drinking late
We picked our way below the wall
But in the higher grass, dewed wet,
Stumbled on tricycle and ball.

When everything was moved away,
The house returned to board and shelf,
And smelt of hot dust through the day,
The garden fell back on itself.

All Night, Legs Pointed East

All night, legs pointed East, I shift around
Inside myself, to breast to crotch to head.
Or freed from catnaps to the teeming night
I float, and pinpoint the minutest sound.
I don't know why I doze my time in bed.

An air moves in, I catch the damp plain smells.
But outside, after winter's weeks of rain
The soil of gardens breaks and dries a bit:
A trough between two San Francisco hills
Where granules hold warmth round them as they drain.

Tonight reminds me of my teens in spring—
Not sexual really, it's a plant's unrest
Or bird's expectancy, that enters full
On its conditions, quick eye claw and wing
Submitting to its pulse, alert in the nest.

Toward the night's end the body lies back, still,
Caught in mid-turn by sleep however brief.
In stealth I fill and fill it out. At dawn
Like loosened soil that packs a grassy hill
I fill it wholly, here, hungry for leaf.

The Geysers

They are in Sonoma County, California. You could camp anywhere
you wanted in the area for a dollar a day, but it was closed down
in 1973. There was also a bath house, containing hot and cool pools.
It was about seventy years old: it may have originally been open to
the sky, but in the seventies it was roughly covered in with sections
of green corrugated plastic.

Thou hast thy walkes for health, as well as sport.

1. *Sleep by the Hot Stream*

Gentle as breathing
                        down to us it spills
From geysers heard but hidden in the hills.
Those starlit scalps are parched blond; where we lie,
The small flat patch of earth fed evenly
By warmth and wet, there's dark grass fine as hair.

This is our bedroom, where we learn the air,
Our sleeping bags laid out in the valley's crotch.
I lie an arm-length from the stream and watch
Arcs fading between stars. There
                        bright! faint! gone!
More meteors than I've ever set eyes on:
The flash-head vanishing as it is defined,
Its own end streaking like a wake behind.

I must have been asleep when morning came.
The v-sides of our shadowed valley frame
The tall hill fair with sunshine opposite.
Live-oaks are of it yet crest separate,
In heavy festooned arches. Now it's day
We get up naked as we intend to stay.

Gentle as breathing
                        Sleep by the hot stream, broken.
Bright, faint, and gone. What I am now has woken.

21

2. *The Cool Stream*

People are wading up the stream all day,
People are swimming, people are at play.

Two birds like one dart upstream toward the falls,
A keen brown thrust between the canyon walls.

Those walls are crammed with neighbouring detail,
Small as an ocean rock-pool's, and no more frail:
Pigmy fern groves, a long web slung across
A perilous bush, an emerald fur of moss;
Wherever it is possible, some plant
Growing in crevices or up a slant.

Sun at meridian shines between the walls
And here below, the talking animals
Enter an unclaimed space, like plants and birds,
And fill it out without too many words
Treating of other places they have been.
I see a little snake alert in its skin
Striped head and neck from water, unmoving, reared:
Tongue-flicker, and a fly has disappeared.
What elegance! it does not watch itself.

Above, wet rounded limbs stretched on a shelf,
The rock glimpsed through blond drying wisps of hair.

A little beach and, barking at the air
Then pacing, pacing, a marooned brown dog.

And some are trying to straddle a floating log,
Some rest and pass a joint, some climb the fall:
Tan black and pink, firm shining bodies, all
Move with a special unconsidered grace.
For though we have invaded this glittering place
And broke the silences, yet we submit:
So wholly, that we are details of it.

3. *The Geyser*

Heat from the sky, and from the rubble of stones.

The higher the more close-picked are Earth's bones:
A climb through moonland, tortured pocked and grey.
Beside the steep path where I make my way
Small puffs of steam bloom out at intervals,
And hot deposit seeps from soggy holes
Scabbing to yellow or wet reddish brown.

I reach the top: the geyser on the crown
Which from the distance was a smart panache
Is merely a searing column of steam from ash.

A cinderfield that lacks all skin of soil,
It has no complication, no detail,
The force too simple and big to comprehend,
Like a beginning, also like an end.
No customs I have learned can make me wise
To deal with such. And I do recognize
—For what such recognition may be worth—
Fire at my centre, burning since my birth
Under the pleasant flesh. Force calls to force.
Up here a man might shrivel in his source.

4. *The Bath House*

Night
    heat
        the hot bath, barely endurable.
Closer than that rank sulphurous smell
a sharp-sweet drifting fume of dope.
Down from half-lucent roofing   moonrays slope
(by the plastic filtered green)
                       to candleflicker below.
Water brims at my chin
                breath coming slow

All round me faces bob   old men, pubescent girls
sweat rolls down foreheads from wet curls
bodies locked soft in trance of heat   not saying much
eyes empty
                    Other senses breaking down to touch
touch of skin   of hot water on the skin
I grasp my mind
                    squeeze open
                              touch within

And grope
          it is hazy suddenly
                              it is strange
          labouring through uneasy change
whether toward ecstasy or panic
                              wish I knew

no longer know for certain who is who
Am I supposed to recognize
those bearded boys   or her, with dreaming eyes

..   ..

Not certain
          who I am or where
weight of a darker earlier air

the body heavily buoyant
                              sheathed by heat
hard, almost, with it
                    Upward, from my feet
I feel rise in me a new kind of blood
The water round me thickens to hot mud
Sunk in it
                    passive   plated   slow
stretching my coils on coils
                              And still I grow
and barely move in years I am so great

I exist I hardly can be said to wait

Till waking one night I look up to see
new gods are shining over me
        What flung Orion's belt across the sky?
I lived the age of reptiles out
                        and I

 . .   . .

lighten, diminish
                in the dream, halfdream
halfdream, reality
                of flickering stream

beneath mud
                branching
                        branching streams run through
through me
                the mud breathes
                                breathes me too

and bobbing in the womb, all round me Mother
I am part of all   there is no other
I extend into
                her mind   her mountainous knees
red meadows   salty seas
birdbone and pulp, unnamed, unborn
                                I live

 . .   . .

It tore
        what flash cut
                        made me fugitive
caesarian lightning lopped me off separate

and born in flight from the world
                                but through it, into it
aware now (piercingly)
                        of my translation
each sense raw-healed   in sudden limitation

I hurry, what I did I do not know
nor who pursues, nor why I go
I crawl along moon-dappled tunnels
                              climb
look back:
              they marked me all the time
shadows that lengthen over whitened fields below
calm, closing in
                    Not all the plants that grow
thickets of freckled foxglove, rank hedgerow,
bowed bushes, laurel, woods of oak could hide me
But now
          I see the stream that bends beside me

quiet and deep, a refuge I could stay within
reminding me of somewhere I have been

hearing their tread
                    I dive in
                              sink beneath
wait hid in
              cool security
                              I cannot breathe
I burst for oxygen
shoot upward, then
break through
              another surface
                              where I meet
 ..   ..

dreamers
          the faces bobbing round me on the heat
green moonlight, smell of dope
                              the shining arms   and eyes
staring at me without surprise
I am trapped
              It will begin
pubescent girl and bearded boy close in

I give up
        hope   as they move in on me

loosened so quickly from it   I am free

I brace myself light strong and clear
and understand why I came here

entering their purpose as they enter mine

I am part of all
        hands take
                hands tear and twine

I yielded
     oh, the yield
             what have I slept?
my blood is yours   the hands that take accept

. .   . .

torn from the self
         in which I breathed and trod
I am

    I am raw meat

        I am a god

Three Songs

Baby Song

From the private ease of Mother's womb
I fall into the lighted room.

Why don't they simply put me back
Where it is warm and wet and black?

But one thing follows on another.
Things were different inside Mother.

Padded and jolly I would ride
The perfect comfort of her inside.

They tuck me in a rustling bed
—I lie there, raging, small, and red.

I may sleep soon, I may forget,
But I won't forget that I regret.

A rain of blood poured round her womb,
But all time roars outside this room.

Hitching into Frisco

Truck put me off on Fell.
I'll walk to Union Square
And watch the homeless there
From jailhouse and hotel.

And liable to none.
I've heard the long freight trains,
The cars marked with home names.
Mom wouldn't know her son.

I was a gentle boy.
That dusty Texas town
Was good for settling down.
The girls were clean and coy.

Had everywhere to go,
And thumbed around the nation.
It's like improvisation
Inside a tune you know.

The highways in the bone
Phrase after phrase unwind.
For all I leave behind
There is a new song grown.

And everywhere to go.

Sparrow

> Chill to the marrow
> pity poor Sparrow
> got any change Sir
> Sparrow needs change Sir

I stand here in the cold
in a loose old suit bruised and dirty
I may look fifty years old
but I'm only thirty

My feet smell bad and they ache
the wine's gone sour and stale in my pores
my throat is sand I shake
and I live out of doors

I shelter from the rain
in a leaky doorway in leaky shoes
and there is only pain
I've got left to lose

I need some change for a drink
of sweet wine Sir a bottle of sherry
it's the sugar in it I think
will make me merry

I'll be a daredevil then
millionaire stud in my right mind
a jewel among men
if you'll be so kind

The bastard passed me by
fuck you asshole that's what I say
I hope I see you cry
like Sparrow one day

2

... and when he pictured in his mind the ugly chamber, false and quiet, false and quiet through the dark hours of two nights, and the tumbled bed, and he not in it, though believed to be, he became in a manner his own ghost and phantom, and was at once the haunting spirit and the haunted man.

Martin Chuzzlewit

The Plunge

down a rope of
bubbles

trapped where you
chose to come
              it
is all there is

the brute thrust of
entering this all-
alien like a bitter
sheath
        each
nerve each
atom of skin
tightens against it
to a gliding
a moving with—
if flesh could
become water it

unlost
        plying
a blurred sunken sky where
you carry your own
pale home with you

at rest in your own
prolonged ache

and the testing forward
how much more can the body
take, how much dare
it is all there is

till
the body
knows now it's
time, lets go ah
holding
almost till too late
gives itself to the slow
rejection
you go limp on it, a
gentle lift, you
wait on it, wait
you

eat the air

Bringing to Light

powder, chunks of road, twisted
skeletal metal, clay
        I think
of ancient cities of bringing to light
foundations under the foundations

bringing a raft of tiny
cellars to light of day:
gold pocks in the
broad sunlight, craters
like a honeycomb bared

. .   . .   . .

In one cellar, a certain mannekin
terribly confined
in his sweat and beard
went crazy as Bothwell.
In another, his jailer lived,
here are his shelves for
cup and smock. He was a jailer
so knew he was free.

. .   . .   . .

Every day the luminous tiers
of the city are filmed with a dust,
a light silt from foot and flesh
and the travelling mind.

. .   . .   . .

I have forgotten a picnic on a hill
in Kent when I was six, but

have a page of snapshots about it.
It still takes place, but in
a cellar I cannot locate.

There is a cellar, a cell, a cellular
room where a handsome spirit
of wilfulness picnics with me
all day limber imaginary brother
dandling me between his feet
kissing my eyes and mouth
and genitals making me
all his own all day
                          as he is mine.

..   ..   ..

But beneath the superior cellars
others reach downward
                          floor under
floor Babel reversed

Opening doors I discover
the debris of sorcery interrupted
    bone structures like experiments

fewer and fewer
joining each other in their origins

separate words return to their roots
lover and mother melt into
one figure that covers its face
nameless and inescapable

need arrayed like a cause

Achilles and Achelous the rivergod
he fought unite in person
and in name as the earlier
Achelous who precedes both

tress of the Greek's hair red-glinting
braids with thick riverweed
the cell darkens with braiding
toward their common root
in the lowest the last the
first cavern, dark and moist
of which
            the foundations
are merely the Earth

..   ..   ..

nothing
        but a faint
smell, mushroomy, thin
as if something
                even here
were separating from its dam

a separating
                of cells

37

Thomas Bewick

I think of a man on foot
going through thick woods,
a buckle on his brimmed hat,
a stick in his hand.

He comes on from the deep
shadow now to the gladed parts
where light speckles the ground
like scoops out of darkness.

Gnarled branches reaching down
their green gifts; weed reaching up
milky flower and damp leaf.

I think of a man fording
a pebbly stream. A rock
is covered in places with
minute crops of moss
—frail stalks of yellow rising
from the green, each
bloom of it distinct, as
he notices. He notices
the bee's many-jointed legs and its
papery wings veined like leaf,
or the rise of a frog's back
into double peaks, and this morning
by a stile he noticed ferns
afloat on air.

Drinking from
clear stream and resting
on the rock he loses himself

in detail,
        he reverts
to an earlier self, not yet
separate from what it sees,

a selfless self as difficult
to recover and hold as to
capture the exact way
a burly bluetit grips
its branch (leaning forward)
over this rock
          and in
The History of British Birds.

Wrestling

(for Robert Duncan)

Discourse
          of sun and moon
fire and beginnings

behind words
          the illuminated words

A palimpsest
          the discourse having been
          erased and replaced with
          words of a role
          but if you hold
          the parchment to light
          you may see
                    the discourse
          where the stylus pressed
          the fat, where it has
          always held, continuing
          luminous behind.
          the covering script
          transparent to it.
          no secret
                    clear,
          still, like a high
          window you never noticed
          it lets in light

continuous discourse
          of angels
          and sons of angels
          of semen, of beginnings
lucid accounts of flight
          arms for wings

a tale of wrestling with a stranger
        a stranger, like
        a man, like

a messenger
        loping, compact
        in familiar places
        he moves with that
        separate grace, that
        sureness of foot
        you know in
        animal and angel

messages from
        sun and moon
picked up
        on waves, interpreted

the sun and moon, for
        signs, for seasons
        hang in darkness
        visible mysteries
        fire
        and reflected fire

language of
        tides and seasons
luminous discourse
        telling about
        beginnings

The Outdoor Concert

At the edge
of the understanding:
      it's the secret.

You recognize not
the content of it but
the fact that it is
there to be recognized.

Dust raised
by vendors and dancers
shimmers on the windless air
where it hovers
as if it will never settle.

The secret
is still the secret

is not a proposition:
it's in finding
what connects the man
with the music, with
the listeners, with the fog
in the top of the eucalyptus,
with dust discovered on the lip

and then in living a while
at that luminous intersection,
spread at the centre
like a white garden spider
so still
that you think it
has become its web,

a god existing
only in its creation.

Saturnalia

The time of year comes
round, the campagna
is stone and grey stalk

Once again outlaws
in majority, the throng
bursts from street to
street
      one body
no longer creeping through
a conduit of mossed stone
or marble it is a
muscled flood, still
rising still reshaping

license awakes us

finding our likeness in
being bare, we
have thrown off
the variegated stuffs that
distinguished us one from
one
      here in orgy
a Laocoon of twined
limbs, in open
incest reaching through to
ourselves in others

beloved flesh

the whole body pulses
like an erection, blood
in the head and furious

with tenderness
                the senses
mingle, before returning
sharpened to their homes,
they roam at play through
each organ as if
each were
             equally
a zone of Eros

Faustus Triumphant

The dazzled blood
submits, carries the
flame through me to every
organ till blood itself
is flamy
       flame animates me
with delight in time's things
so intense that I am
almost lost to time

Already vining the
arbours of my body, flame
starts from my fingers!
now my flame-limbs wrap round
marble   ebony   fur   flesh
without combusting what
they embrace. I
lick everything.
               What
tracks led

      There.
and there and there
where I pricked the
arm where I
got the blood to sign

I remember there was
a bargain made but I
think I'm safe. For
vein and artery are not
store keepers, nor is
Nature a lawyer.

My joy so great
that if hell threatens, the
memory alone of flame
protects me. There is
no terror in combustion.
I shall rejoice to
enter into him
                    Father-
Nature, the Great Flame

Dolly

You recognize it like
the smell of the sour chemical
that gets into the sweat
of some people from
birth onward.

        And you say
he's out to end his choices
for good and doesn't realize it.

I know someone who
was never let play with dolls
when he was little, so now
(he thinks to spite his father)
collects them.
But it's the crippled ones
he cherishes most, particularly
the quadriplegics: they loll
blank stomachs depending from blank heads
with no freedom
            ever, ever

and in need.

Jack Straw's Castle

I.

Jack Straw sits
        sits in his castle
Jack Straw watches the rain

why can't I leave my castle
he says, isn't there anyone
anyone here besides me

sometimes I find myself wondering
if the castle is castle at all
a place apart, or merely
the castle that every snail
must carry around till his death

and then there's the matter of breath
on a cold day it rears before me
like a beautiful fern
I'm amazed at the plant

will it survive me
a man of no account
visited only by visions

and no one here
no one who knows how to play

visions, voices, burning smells
all of a rainy day

2.

Pig Pig she cries
I can hear her from next door
He fucked me in the mouth
and now he won't give me car fare
she rages and cries

3.

The rain stops. I look round: a square of floor,
Blond wood, shines palely in the laggard sun;
The kittens suck, contrasting strips of fur,
The mother in their box, a perfect fit,
I finally got it how I wanted it,
A fine snug house when all is said and done.

But night makes me uneasy: floor by floor
Rooms never guessed at open from the gloom
First as thin smoky lines, ghost of a door
Or lintel that develops like a print
Darkening into full embodiment
—Boudoir and oubliette, room on room on room.

And I have met or I believed I met
People in some of them, though they were not
The kind I need. They looked convincing, yet
There always was too much of the phantom to them.
Meanwhile, and even when I walked right through them,
I was talking, talking to myself. Of what?

Fact was, the echo of each word drowned out
The next word spoken, and I cannot say
What it was I was going on about.
It could be I was asking, Do these rooms
Spring up at night-time suddenly, like mushrooms,
Or have they all been hiding here all day?

4·

Dream sponsors:
Charles Manson, tongue
playing over dry lips,
thinking a long thought;
and the Furies, mad
puppety heads appearing
in the open transom above
a forming door, like heads
of kittens staring angrily
over the edge of their box:

'Quick, fetch Medusa,'
their shrewish voices,
'Show him Medusa.'

Maybe I won't turn away,
maybe I'm so cool
I could outstare her.

5·

The door opens.
There are no snakes.
The head
is on the table.

On the table
gold hair struck
by light from
the naked bulb,
a dazzle in which
the ground of dazzle
is consumed, the
hair burning
in its own gold.

And her eyes
gaze at me,
pale blue, but
blank as the eyes
of zombie or angel,
with the stunned
lack of expression
of one
who has beheld
the source of everything
and found it
the same as nothing.

In her dazzle I
catch fire
self-delighting
self-sufficient
self-consuming
till
I burn out
so heavy
I sink into
darkness into
my foundations.

6.

Down in the cellars, nothing is visible
                              no one
Though there's a sound about me of many breathing
Light slap of foot on stone and rustle of body
Against body and stone.
                    And when later
I finger a stickiness along the ridges
Of a large central block that feels like granite
I don't know if it's my own, or I shed it,
Or both, as if priest and victim were only

Two limbs of the same body.
                              The lost traveller.
For this is the seat of needs
                    so deep, so old
That even where eye never perceives body
And where the sharpest ear discerns only
The light slap and rustle of flesh on stone
They, the needs, seek ritual and ceremony
To appease themselves
                    (Oh, the breathing all around me)
Or they would tear apart the life that feeds them.

7.

I am the man on the rack.
I am the man who puts the man on the rack.
I am the man who watches the man who puts the man on the
                                                        rack.

8.

Might it not have been
a thought-up film
which suddenly ceases

the lights go up
I can see only
this pearl-grey chamber
false and quiet
no audience here
just the throned one

nothing outside the bone
nothing accessible

the ambush and taking of
meaning were nothing
                              were
inventions of Little Ease

I sit
trapped in bone
I am back again
where I never left, I sit
in my first instant, where
I never left

petrified at my centre

9.

I spin like a solitary star, I swoon.

But there breaks into my long solitude

A bearded face, it's Charlie, close as close,
His breath that stinks of jail—of pain and fungus,
So close that I breathe nothing else.

Then I recall as if it were my own
Life on the hot ranch, and the other smells.
Of laurel in the sun, fierce, sweet; of people
—Death-sweat or lust-sweat they smelt much the same.
He reigned in sultry power over his dream.

I come back to the face pushed into mine.
Tells me he's bound to point out, man,
That dreams don't come from nowhere: it's your dream
He says, you dreamt it. So there's no escape.

And now he's squatting at a distance
To wait the taunt's effect, paring his nails,
From time to time glancing up sideways at me,
A sly mad look. Yes, but he's not mad either.

He's gone too far, Charlie you've overdone it.
Something inside my head turns over.
I think I see how his taunt can be my staircase,
For if I brought all of this stuff inside
There must be an outside to bring it from.
Outside the castle, somewhere, there must be
A real Charles Manson, a real woman crying,
And laws I had no hand in, like gravity.

About midnight. Where earlier there had seemed
A shadowy arch projected on the bone-like stone,
I notice, fixing itself,
Easing itself in place even as I see it,
A staircase leading upward.
                                   Is that rain
Far overhead, that drumming sound?
Boy, what a climb ahead.

At the bottom, looking back, I find
He is, for now at any rate, clean gone.

10.

My coldness wakes me,
mine, and the kitchen chair's.

How long have I sat here? I
went to sleep in bed.

Entering real rooms perhaps,
my own spectre, cold,

unshivering as a flight of
flint steps that leads nowhere,

in a ruin, where the wall
abruptly ends, and the steps too

and you stare down at the broken
slabs far below, at the ivy

glinting over bone-chips which must
at one time have been castle.

II.

Down panic, down. The castle is still here,
And I am in the kitchen with a beer
Hearing the hurricane thin out to rain.
Got to relax if I'm to sleep again.
The castle is here, but not snug any more,
I'm loose, I rattle in its hollow core.
And as for that parade of rooms—shed, jail,
Cellar, each snapping at the next one's tail—
That raced inside my skull for half the night,
I hope I'm through with that. I flick the light.
And though the dungeon will be there for good
(What laid those stones?) at least I found I could,
Thrown down, escape by learning what to learn;
And hold it that held me.
                                        Till I return.

And so to bed, in hopes that I won't dream.

  ..   ..

I drift, doze, sleep. But toward dawn it does seem,
While I half-wake, too tired to turn my head,
That someone stirs behind me in the bed
Between two windows on an upper floor.
Is it a real man muttering? I'm not sure.
Though he does not seem phantom-like as yet,
Thick, heavily breathing, with a sweet faint sweat.

So humid, we lie sheetless—bare and close,
Facing apart, but leaning ass to ass.

And that mere contact is sufficient touch,
A hinge, it separates but not too much.
An air moves over us, as calm and cool
As the green water of a swimming pool.

What if this is the man I gave my key
Who got in while I slept? Or what if he,
Still, is a dream of that same man?
                                    No, real.
Comes from outside the castle, I can feel.
The beauty's in what is, not what may seem.
I turn. And even if he were a dream
—Thick sweating flesh against which I lie curled—
With dreams like this, Jack's ready for the world.

1973–4

An Amorous Debate

Leather Kid and Fleshly

Birds whistled, all
Nature was doing something while
Leather Kid and Fleshly
lay on a bank and
gleamingly discoursed
                        like this:
'You are so strong,' she said, 'such
a firm defense of hide against
the ripple of skin, it
excites me, all those
reserves suggested, though I do hope
that isn't a prosthetic device
under your glove is it?'

'Let's fuck,' he said.

She snuggled close, zipping
him open, unbuckling away
till he lay before her
                        a very
Mars unhorsed but
not doing much of
anything without his horse.

'Strange,' she said, 'you
are still encased in your
defense. You have
a hard cock but there is
something like the
obduracy of leather
still in your countenance
and your skin, it is like
a hide under hide.'
Then she laid the fierce

pale river of her body
against his, squashing
her lily breasts against
his hard male nipples, inserting
her thighs between his till
he fired a bit and
embracing her with some feeling
moved his head to suck at
the nearest flesh to
his mouth which turned out
to be his own arm.

Then a tremor passed
through his body, the sheen
fell from him, he
became wholly sensitive
as if his body had
rolled back its own foreskin.
(He began to sweat.)

And they melted one
into the other
    forthwith
like the way the Saône
joins the Rhône at Lyon.

3

Autobiography

The sniff of the real, that's
what I'd want to get
        how it felt
to sit on Parliament
Hill on a May evening
studying for exams   skinny
seventeen   dissatisfied
        yet sniffing such
a potent air, smell of
grass in heat from
the day's sun

I'd been walking through the damp
rich ways by the ponds
and now lay on the upper
grass with Lamartine's poems

life seemed all
loss, and what was more
I'd lost whatever it was
before I'd even had it

a green dry prospect
distant babble of children
and beyond, distinct at
the end of the glow
St Paul's like a stone thimble

longing so hard to make
inclusions that the longing
has become   in memory
an inclusion

Hampstead: the Horse Chestnut Trees

At the top of a low hill
two stand together, green
bobbings contained within
the general sway. They
must be about my age.
My brother and I
rode between them and
down the hill and the impetus
took us on without pedalling
to be finally braked by
a bit of sullen marsh
(no longer there) where the mud
was coloured by the red-brown
oozings of iron. It
was autumn
                or was it?

Nothing to keep it there, the
smell of leaf in May
sweet and powerful as rutting
confuses me now, it's all
getting lost, I started
forgetting it even as I wrote.

Forms remain, not the life
of detail or hue
then the forms are lost and
only a few dates stay with you.

But the trees have no sentiments
their hearts are wood
and preserve nothing
                      their
boles get great, they are

embraced by the wind they
rushingly embrace,
they spread outward
and upward
                without regret
hardening tender green
to insensate lumber.

The Roadmap

If I saw you liked that dull unhappy boy
and let you be, and did not react
to see you driving off together
to the country on Sundays
                    it was
to make your position indefensible
and, that established,
must not my own lack of blame
survive, copious?
(How can you answer back? You were in the wrong.)

I teased a schoolmaster when I was twelve
until his accumulated rage
was out of proportion to the offence.
Thus, I reasoned, there could be no offence.
My emotions drew up a roadmap.

Now my mind catches up and looks back.

And wreckages of trust litter the route
each an offence against me.
I gaze back
            in hardened innocence.

The Idea of Trust

The idea of trust, or,
the thief. He
was always around,
'pretty' Jim.
Like a lilac bush or
a nice picture on the wall.
Blue eyes of an
intense vagueness
and the well-arranged
bearing of an animal.
Then one day he
said something!
     he said
that trust is
an intimate conspiracy.

What did that
mean? Anyway next day
he was gone, with
all the money and dope
of the people he'd lived with.

I begin
to understand. I see him
picking through their things
at his leisure, with
a quiet secret smile
choosing and taking,
having first discovered
and set up his phrase to
scramble
that message of
enveloping trust.

He's getting
free. His eyes
are almost transparent.
He has put on
gloves. He fingers
the little privacies of those
who acted as if there
should be no privacy.

They took that
risk.
    Wild lilac
chokes the garden.

Courage, a Tale

There was a Child
who heard from another Child
that if you masturbate 100 times
it kills you.

This gave him pause;
he certainly slowed down quite a bit
and also
        kept count.

But, till number 80,
was relatively loose about it.
There did seem plenty of time left.

The next 18
were reserved for celebrations,
like the banquet room in a hotel.

The 99th time
was simply unavoidable.

Weeks passed.

And then he thought
Fuck it
        it's worth dying for,

and half an hour later
the score rose from 99 to 105.

Behind the Mirror

1.

Once in a dark restaurant I caught the eyes of another,
they stared back at mine with unflagging interest.
Another! no it was my own eyes from a recessed mirror.

I and the reflected self seemed identical twins,
alike yet separate, two flowers from the same plant.

2.

Narcissus glares into the pool: someone glares back.
As he leans over the surface, absorbed, he sees
only the other—he sees the rounded arms,
a hunk of auburn hair tumbled forward, lips parted
in awe, in craving: he stares him
straight in the ravenous eyes
                              and reaches down toward him.

He escapes, he does not escape, he is the same, he is other.
If he drowned himself he would be one with himself.
If he drowned himself he would wash free into the world,
placid and circular, from which he has been withdrawn.
He would at last be of it, deep behind the mirror,
white limbs braided with a current
where both water and earth are part of it,
and would come to rest on a soft dark wave of soil
to root there and stand again
                              one flower,
one waxy star, giving perfume, unreflecting.

The Cherry Tree

In her gnarled sleep it
begins
        though she seems
as unmoving as the statue
of a running man: her
branches caught in a
writhing, her trunk
leaning as if in mid-fall.
When the wind moves
against her grave body
only the youngest twigs
scutter amongst themselves.

But there's something going on
in those twisted brown limbs,
it starts as a need
and it takes over, a need
to push
        push outward
from the centre, to
bring what is not
from what is, pushing
till at the tips of the push
something comes about
                            and then
pulling it from outside
until yes she has them started
tiny bumps
appear at the ends of twigs.

Then at once they're all here,
she wears them like a coat
a coat of babies,
I almost think that she

preens herself, jubilant at
the thick dazzle of bloom,
that the caught writhing has become
a sinuous wriggle of joy
beneath her fleece.
But she is working still
to feed her children,
there's a lot more yet,
bringing up all she can
a lot of goodness from roots

while the petals drop.
The fleece is gone
as suddenly as it came
and hundreds of babies are left
almost too small to be seen
but they fatten, fatten, get pink
and shine among her leaves.

Now she can repose a bit
they are so fat.
                    She cares less
birds get them, men
pick them, human children wear them
in pairs over their ears
she loses them all.
That's why she made them,
to lose them into the world, she
returns to herself,
she rests, she doesn't care.

She leans into the wind
her trunk shines black
with rain, she sleeps
as black and hard as lava.
She knows nothing about babies.

Mandrakes

look for us among those
shy flowers opening
at night only
             in the
shadow, in the held breath
under oak trees listen for

rootshuffle or is it wind
    you won't find us, we
got small a long time back
we withdrew like the Picts
into fireside tale and rumour

we were terrible in our time
gaunt plants fertilized
by the leachings of hanged men
    knobby frames shrieking and
stumping around the planet

smaller and bushier now
prudent green men moving
in oakshadow or among reed
guardians of the young snake
             rearing from the water
             with the head and curving
             neck of a small dinosaur

we can outwait you for
ever if we need, lounging
leafy arms linked along
some park's path, damp fallen leaves
covering our itch to move

mouths open to the wind
sigh entering the sough
from the distant branches

like a rumour at your fireside

Yoko

All today I lie in the bottom of the wardrobe
feeling low but sometimes getting up
to moodily lumber across rooms
and lap from the toilet bowl, it is so sultry
and then I hear the noise of firecrackers again
all New York is jaggedy with firecrackers today
and I go back to the wardrobe gloomy
trying to void my mind of them.
I am confused, I feel loose and unfitted.

At last deep in the stairwell I hear a tread,
it is him, my leader, my love.
I run to the door and listen to his approach.
Now I can smell him, what a good man he is,
I love it when he has the sweat of work on him,
as he enters I yodel with happiness,
I throw my body up against his, I try to lick his lips,
I care about him more than anything.

After we eat we go for a walk to the piers.
I leap into the standing warmth, I plunge into
the combination of old and new smells.
Here on a garbage can at the bottom, so interesting,
what sister or brother I wonder left this message I sniff.
I too piss there, and go on.
Here a hydrant there a pole
here's a smell I left yesterday, well that's disappointing
but I piss there anyway, and go on.
I investigate so much that in the end
it is for form's sake only, only a drop comes out.

I investigate tar and rotten sandwiches, everything, and go on.

And here a dried old turd, so interesting
so old, so dry, yet so subtle and mellow.

1 can place it finely, I really appreciate it,
a gold distant smell like packed autumn leaves in winter
reminding me how what is rich and fierce when excreted
becomes weathered and mild
                            but always interesting
and reminding me of what I have to do.

My leader looks on and expresses his approval.

I sniff it well and later I sniff the air well
a wind is meeting us after the close July day
rain is getting near too but first the wind.

Joy, joy,
being outside with you, active, investigating it all,
with bowels emptied, feeling your approval
and then running on, the big fleet Yoko,
my body in its excellent black coat never lets me down,
returning to you (as I always will, you know that)
and now
            filling myself out with myself, no longer confused,
my panting pushing apart my black lips, but unmoving,
I stand with you braced against the wind.

The Release

And I assemble it as it was when I walked on it,
the street, it's unstable, that's what keeps me going,
the sense of mild but constant risk.

I watch him in my mind, the man I saw,
something odd and off-balance about him:
the forward lifted eyes the forward leaning walk,
his yellowish hair bouncing behind him as he walks,
he is beautiful, eager—maybe speeding a little
—with a constant vague air of slight surprise.

With the same hurrying slouch he turns the corner as he did
and as he did he sits on some house-steps in the sun.
He eases to and fro in his consciousness,
he moves in and out of my poem.

What am I doing to this man in the yellow jacket?
Reading him, pretending he is legible,
thinking I can master what is self-contained.
I know only his outer demeanour, his clothing and his skin,
and presume an inner structure I can never be sure of.
I must return to him as he was,
a shimmering planet sheathed in its own air.

The hair on his shoulders stirring in a light wind
he sits on somebody else's front steps and hugs his knees
and stares glowingly ahead as he plans some slightly stoned plan:

he's unpredictable, clean of me
(he never notices me as I stare freely).
I must try to leave him as I found him, and so

as if suddenly resolving something
he suddenly unfixes his eyes, jumps to his feet
and slouches eagerly back to the street he came from.

Breaking Ground

1. *Kent*

Lank potato, darkening
cabbage, tattered raspberry
canes, but the flower beds
so crammed there is
no room for weeds
    fiercely aflame all August
when I sniff at the bergamot
the fruity-sage smell is like
a flower sweating

she's too old now to
dig, too old to move
that barrow of cuttings
by the shed, some
nephew can move it

barrow of cuttings, of
grasses not yet hay, fresh
green of redundant
branch, and nasturtium
only rusted a little at
edges of hot yellow

going down to earth, that's
what I can't accept
her kind hand, her
grey eyes, her voice
intonations I've known
all my life—to be
lost, forgotten in
an indiscriminate mulch, a
humus of no colour

2. *Monterey*

Looking down on the stage
from side-bleachers, my mind heavy

October and high fog
Joan Baez singing
Let it Be, during which
a break comes in the sky

and in the crowd below
detail after detail comes
alive, a repeated
movement of stretching arms,
people all over taking off
their coats and shirts,
patches of flesh-colour
start out from the khaki
and grey background

what flashes of warm
skin, what a blooming
of body
   firm
and everlasting petals

Let it be. It
comes to me at last that
when she dies she
loses indeed
that sweet character, loses
all self, and
is dispersed—but dispersal
means
   spreading abroad:

she is not still contained
in the one person, she
is distributed
through fair warm flesh

of strangers
—some have her touch, some
her eyes, some her
voice, never to be
forgotten: renewed again
and again throughout
one great garden which
is always here.
                    Shee
is gonn, Shee is lost,
Shee is found, shee
is ever faire.

Acknowledgements

The poems in this book first appeared in the following publications: *Agenda, Antaeus, Blackfish, Chicago Review, Gay News, Iowa Review, Isthmus, Listener, Occident, Open Reading, Sequoia, Thames Poetry,* and *Unmuzzled Ox.* Some first appeared in the following limited editions: *Jack Straw's Castle* (Frank Hallman), *Mandrakes* illustrated by Leonard Baskin (Rainbow Press), *Songbook* illustrated by Bill S. (Albondocani Press), and *To the Air* (David R. Godine). 'All Night, Legs Pointed East' was first published as a Christmas card for the Albondocani Press, 'Last Days at Teddington' appeared as a *Poem of the Month*, and 'The Cherry Tree' was in the *New Yorker.* The last part of 'The Geysers' was printed in a different version in *New Departures*; 'Jack Straw's Castle' in a shorter and different version in *Manroot*.